VOLUME SIX

Heaven Speaks to Families

Direction for Our Times
As given to Anne,
a lay apostle

VOLUME SIX

Direction for Our Times
As given to Anne, a lay apostle

ISBN: 978-0-976684-15-2

Library of Congress Number: Applied For

Publisher:
Direction for Our Times
9000 West 81st Street
Justice, IL 60458

708-496-9300
www.directionforourtimes.org

Direction for Our Times is a 501(c)(3) tax-exempt organization.

Manufactured in the United States of America

Graphic Design: Pete Massari

How to Pray the Rosary information and the image of Our Lady Immaculate are used with permission. Copyright © Congregation of Marians of the Immaculate Conception, Stockbridge, MA 01263. www.marian.org.

Copy of painting of *Jesus Christ the Returning King* by Janusz Antosz

Direction for Our Times wishes to manifest its complete obedience and submission of mind and heart to the final and definitive judgment of the Magisterium of the Catholic Church and the local Ordinary regarding the supernatural character of the messages received by Anne, a lay apostle.

In this spirit, the messages of Anne, a lay apostle, have been submitted to her bishop, Most Reverend Leo O'Reilly, Bishop of Kilmore, Ireland, and to the Vatican Congregation for the Doctrine of the Faith for formal examination. In the meantime Bishop O'Reilly has given permission for their publication.

Table of Contents

Part Four

Introduction

Dear Reader,

I am a wife, mother of six, and a Secular Franciscan.

At the age of twenty, I was divorced for serious reasons and with pastoral support in this decision. In my mid-twenties I was a single parent, working and bringing up a daughter. As a daily Mass communicant, I saw my faith as sustaining and had begun a journey toward unity with Jesus, through the Secular Franciscan Order or Third Order.

My sister travelled to Medjugorje and came home on fire with the Holy Spirit. After hearing of her beautiful pilgrimage, I experienced an even more profound conversion. During the following year I experienced various levels of deepened prayer, including a dream of the Blessed Mother, where she asked me if I would work for Christ. During the dream she showed me that this special spiritual work would mean I would be separated from others in the world. She actually showed me my extended family and how I would be separated from them. I told her that I did not care. I would do anything asked of me.

Shortly after, I became sick with endometriosis. I have been sick ever since, with one thing or another. My sicknesses are always the types that mystify doctors in the beginning. This is part of the cross and I mention it because so many suffer in this way. I was told by my doctor that I would never conceive children. As a single parent, this did not concern me as I assumed it was God's will. Soon after, I met a wonderful man. My first marriage had been annulled and we married and conceived five children.

Spiritually speaking, I had many experiences that included what I now know to be interior locutions. These moments were beautiful and the words still stand out firmly in my heart, but I did not get excited because I was busy offering up illnesses and exhaustion. I took it as a matter of course that Jesus had to work hard to sustain me as He had given me a lot to handle. In looking back, I see that He was preparing me to do His work. My preparation period was long, difficult and not very exciting. From the outside, I think people thought, man, that woman has bad luck. From the inside, I saw that while my sufferings were painful and long lasting, my little family was growing in love, in size and in wisdom, in the sense that my husband and I certainly understood what was important and what was not important. Our continued crosses did that for us.

Various circumstances compelled my husband and me to move with our children far from my loved ones. I offered this up and must say it is the most difficult thing I have had to contend with. Living in exile brings many beautiful opportunities to align with Christ's will; however, you have to continually remind yourself that you are doing that. Otherwise you just feel sad. After several years in exile, I finally got the inspiration to go to Medjugorje. It was actually a gift from my husband for my fortieth birthday. I had tried to go once before, but circumstances prevented the trip and I understood it was not God's will. Finally, though, it was time and my eldest daughter and I found ourselves in front of St. James Church. It was her second trip to Medjugorje.

I did not expect or consider that I would experience anything out of the ordinary. My daughter, who loved it on her first trip, made many jokes about people looking for miracles. She affectionately calls Medjugorje a carnival for religious people. She also says it is the happiest place on earth. This young woman initially went there as a rebellious fourteen-year-old, who took the opportunity to travel abroad with her aunt. She returned calm and respectful, prompting my husband to say we would send all our teenagers on pilgrimage.

At any rate, we had a beautiful five days. I experienced a spiritual healing on the mountain. My daughter rested and prayed. A quiet but significant thing happened to me. During my Communions, I spoke with Jesus conversationally. I thought this was beautiful, but it had happened before on occasion so I was not stunned or overcome. I remember telling others that Communions in Medjugorje were powerful. I came home, deeply grateful to Our Lady for bringing us there.

The conversations continued all that winter. At some time in the six months that followed our trip, the conversations leaked into my life and came at odd times throughout the day. Jesus began to direct me with decision and I found it more and more difficult to refuse when He asked me to do this or that. I told no one.

During this time, I also began to experience direction from the Blessed Mother. Their voices are not hard to distinguish. I do not hear them in an auditory way, but in my soul or mind. By this time I knew that something remarkable was occurring and Jesus was telling me that He had special work for me, over and above my primary vocation as wife and mother. He told me to write the messages down and that He would arrange to have them published and disseminated. Looking back, it took Him a long time to get me comfortable enough where I was willing to trust Him. I trust His voice now and will continue to do my best to serve Him, given my constant struggle with weaknesses, faults, and the pull of the world.

Please pray for me as I continue to try to serve Jesus. Please answer "yes" to Him because He so badly needs us and He is so kind. He will take you right into His heart if you let Him. I am praying for you and am so grateful to God that He has given you these words. Anyone who knows Him must fall in love with Him, such is His goodness. If you have been struggling, this is your answer. He is coming to you in a special way through these words and the graces that flow through them.

Please do not fall into the trap of thinking that He cannot possibly mean for you to reach high levels of holiness. As I say somewhere in my writings, the greatest sign of the times is Jesus having to make do with the likes of me as His secretary. I consider myself the B-team, dear friends. Join me and together we will do our little bit for Him.

Message received from Jesus immediately following my writing of the above biographical information:

You see, My child, that you and I have been together for a long time. I was working quietly in your life for years before you began this work. Anne, how I love you. You can look back through your life and see so many "yes" answers to Me. Does that not please you and make you glad? You began to say "yes" to Me long before you experienced extraordinary graces. If you had not, My dearest, I could never have given you the graces or assigned this mission to you. Do you see how important it was that you got up every day, in your ordinary life, and said "yes" to your God, despite difficulty, temptation, and hardship? You could not see the big plan as I saw it. You had to rely on your faith. Anne, I tell you today, it is still that way. You cannot see My plan, which is bigger than your human mind can accept. Please continue to rely on your faith as it brings Me such glory. Look at how much I have been able to do with you, simply because you made a quiet and humble decision for Me. Make another quiet and humble decision on this day and every day, saying, "I will serve God." Last night you served Me by bringing comfort to a soul in pain. You decided against yourself and for Me, through your service to him. There was gladness in Heaven, Anne. You are Mine. I am yours. Stay with Me, My child. Stay with Me.

The Allegiance Prayer
For All Lay Apostles

Dear God in Heaven, I pledge my allegiance to You. I give You my life, my work and my heart. In turn, give me the grace of obeying Your every direction to the fullest possible extent. Amen.

Part One:
Mary, an unknown saint, Speaks to Mothers

Note: Please be careful not to confuse Mary, an unknown saint, with Mary, our Blessed Mother.

June 7, 2004
Mary (an unknown saint) Speaks to Mothers

With gracious permission from the Lord Jesus Christ, I speak today to all mothers. You are living in a time when mothers are no longer honored for the important role they play in the protection and development of society. Mothers, you are the cornerstone of the home and the home is the place where a person's soul begins his or her critical formation. The enemy labors relentlessly to persuade mothers that they should leave the home and abandon the development of their children to others. Mothers, another person cannot love your child the way you love your child. Another person, even though he or she may be a good person, is not intimately interested in the emotional and spiritual development of your child. Many of you must work to support your family. Jesus understands that and will help you, as will I. But you must scrutinize your situation fearlessly and be certain you are leaving your children so that you can earn the money to procure necessities. It will not be acceptable to say you left the rearing of your children to others so that you could earn money that was not needed. I tell you this because our Lord wishes families to be together. Jesus, who knows exactly what each soul requires for proper formation, is asking that mothers remain home with their children whenever possible. I am unknown in your world, yet I am a beloved saint here in Heaven. On earth, I cared for my children in my home. There were many times when I found the work tedious. I can assure you that I often longed to be working outside of my home because I had always thought I would work professionally. The days may seem tedious, dear mothers, but when stitched together they make the most beautiful tapestry that illustrates the growth of a little soul. I earned a very high place in Heaven simply by caring for my husband and children. If you have more than one child, then you are teaching Christ-like behavior all day long as you show the children how to behave toward each other. If this beautiful formation occurs in the home, you will send your children out, knowing that you have helped the Kingdom to release Christ-followers into the troubled world. You may not understand the gravity of your role, but if you meditate on it you will see that if all mothers were to abandon their responsibilities, we would see even greater darkness. Jesus will not allow this, of course. I want to speak to those mothers who have lost children through sickness or tragedy. Dearest mother, whose heart is broken, you will see your child again, and when you do you will see that your child has been joyful and cared for in your brief separation. Do not grieve if you can help it, but spread joy to those who also grieve. Ask me and I will help you to do this because I know that it seems an impossible thing. All is well in Heaven. Have no fear that your child is not with God. We must all cooperate with Heaven during this time, so prayerfully consider what it is that Jesus needs from you.

June 8, 2004
Mary (an unknown saint) Speaks to Mothers

Again, today, I speak to mothers. Jesus, who understands all, wishes that I speak to you with the power of experience. When someone speaks to you about a skill and you suspect that the person knows nothing about the topic he addresses, you tend to wonder why you are listening. But when someone speaks to you with the benefit of experience, you listen more carefully, because if you are wise you will wish to learn from that person's experience and so avoid mistakes you might otherwise make. I wish to help you to understand the noble task of mothering that God has willed for you. If you are a mother, the parenting and direction of your child must be the first priority of each day. You must see to the child's needs before anything else. If you are working in a job where it is not possible that you do this, you must consider carefully whether or not our Lord wishes you to remain in that job. Again I must say that I do not speak to mothers who are working to provide for food and shelter for their children. You will know yourself if you are working from necessity or working from the desire to acquire more worldly possessions than you need. Let us examine what is necessary for a child to flourish in today's world. Food, shelter and clothing are the barest concrete necessities. What kind of food does your child need? Simple food, prepared at home, by someone who loves the child. This is the best way to nourish a growing body. If your child is well used to eating at home and eating simple foods, that child will not demand more elaborate fare. If the child does demand more elaborate fare, you simply say "no." Now we look at shelter. When a child is born and is laid in his mother's arms, he does not wonder how many rooms are in his home. He feels safe and warm and is content. That child is brought home. Again, he is not concerned with how big his house is, rather, he is concerned that when he cries, his mother responds. The child begins to grow and look around. Still, he does not say, "Why don't I have a big house? Why don't I have an expensive car to drive in?" He looks to his parents for guidance in this area and if his parents are content with what that family has, then the child understands that there is no reason to complain. If a parent is discontent and always longing for something better or something more, the child feels he, too, has been shorted. Mothers, please set a tone of thanksgiving for what you have, regardless of how humble are your possessions. Your child will do the same and you will set the course for a lifetime of contentment, rather than a lifetime of greed and covetousness. I must speak about clothing. Again, if you do not entertain thoughts of bitterness that your clothes are not as fine as the next person's, your child will think nothing of it. When he comes home and says that other children have better clothing than he does, you must say that in Heaven nobody looks at clothing and begin to praise the beauty of your child's soul and the lovely virtues that are developing. "My child will not like this," some will say. Again I say to you dear mothers that your child will adopt the tone you set. Set a tone of simplicity in your home and explain to your child that your family rejects the notion that fine clothes and homes make fine people. Holy households make fine people and that is what you must strive for. You will find peace in your home if you try to implement these concepts because you will have all of Heaven assisting you. I understand that some children have been exposed to worldly ideas and we will speak about that tomorrow. For today, concentrate on simplicity in your home.

June 9, 2004
Mary (an unknown saint) Speaks to Mothers

Dear mothers, you must serve tirelessly. Those who have not experienced motherhood cannot understand how hard it can be to work, performing the same tasks over and over. When you perform these tasks in love, great graces can be obtained for both your family and for the Kingdom. In this way you are directly contributing to the advancement of the cause of Heaven. Jesus is so pleased with this kind of cooperative service and He will reward you in countless ways. Cleaning your floors then becomes a divine service, as does washing your dishes, or cleaning the children's clothes, or any of the hundreds of domestic chores you perform daily. I am in Heaven now and I have the benefit of such wisdom and knowledge. You would be overjoyed to see my reward, yet I was a simple housewife. I looked on my role of mother as a serious task. I saw each child individually and wondered where they would fit. I tried to help them develop their strengths, all the while searching for the character flaws that might cause them hardship. When I spotted something I felt might be a problem for them, I tried to help them conquer this flaw. These little acts of control or mortification should be praised in your small ones because as they grow they will then practice that same control or mortification as adults. There is no way to understand the importance of that early formation. Truly, believe me when I tell you that you will see your children as adults behaving the same way they did as children, so if a troublesome behavior is allowed as a child, that individual will practice that same behavior as an adult, only you will have little power to correct it. So watch your children closely and praise their little virtues with great constancy. Praise and encouragement will win the day with little ones. When you do identify that little flaw, mothers, speak softly but firmly and explain how Jesus will help with any temptations. Do not criticize your children in such a way that they are embarrassed, as this is never a good thing and causing a child public shame results in the most serious of effects. But quietly and privately explain why such behavior is wrong and how it could hurt either someone else or the person committing the act. The little soul is so precious and must be preserved. We teach children how to clean themselves and how to feed themselves. We must also teach children how to clean and feed their little souls. Many of today's children do not even know they have a soul, much less how to protect it and maintain it. Poor Jesus. How He looks with sadness upon these precious little ones, so hungry in spiritual terms. Mothers, treat this responsibility with the greatest of reverence. I want to help you. Our

Lady wants to help you. I prayed to her so often and she always helped me. There were many times when I worried myself nearly sick over a child. There was no need for this. I should have trusted more. I urge you all to pray together, but we hardly need talk about the necessity of family prayer. Let me say that there are invisible graces that flow down upon a family during family prayer. Those graces provide unseen ties that hold a family close during all trials. Pretend these ties are visible, and that you can see them flowing down upon your family as you pray together. I want to tell you that when you attempt to introduce family prayer to those children who have not prayed together in the past, you may experience resistance. Expect this. Also, when you say "no" to a child who has previously been given many material things, you will get anger. It will pass. Your child will object to being forced to pray and having material things taken away. Be brave, mothers. Be strong. Do not think for a moment that your decisions should be based on the anger or resistance of your children. Make your decision, and then impose it. Your children will come around if you are firm. Pray to Our Lady to help you turn your household into another holy family that serves the Kingdom. She will hear you and she will help. Set an example of calm holiness yourself and I promise you that all will be well.

June 10, 2004
Mary (an unknown saint) Speaks to Mothers

We must speak today to all mothers who are alone in the parenting of their children. Dear mother, you are supposed to have help, it is true. It is very difficult to be alone in a job that requires two people. Do not be afraid, though, because in this situation Heaven steps in with great power. You must tell yourself to be brave. You will never be alone in any problem that involves your parenting. God is the Father of your children and He has placed them in your care. He will see that you have everything you need to shepherd your children through their childhoods. You must communicate with Him constantly about your fears, your concerns over their development and, of course, providing for their material needs. You should also confide in Mary, the Blessed Mother. She was a constant source of comfort and support to me in my own parenting. Between Jesus and Mary, you will have all of the assistance you require. Please believe that if you are following the path to Heaven, your children will also follow the path to Heaven. A great deal of the work of parenting is done in the example that you set. If you walk constantly toward Christ, your children will recognize that path, and they will recognize when they have left that path. You are not a single parent, dear mother, because you are part of a heavenly team that is going to see that your children receive exactly what they need to serve Christ. You have many friends in Heaven who understand your struggles. Cry out to them when you are worried. When you experience joy and there is nobody there to share it with you, share it with Jesus. He will experience such delight if you do this. Our Jesus wants people to rely on Him in grief, of course, but He takes special joy in a soul calling Him in to share family happiness or accomplishment. This will create for Jesus a firm role in your family and He will not disappoint you or fail to pull His share of the weight. Such a thing is not possible. You must always remember this, dear little mother who feels so afraid at times. You are not alone. Speak constantly to Heaven about your children. Heaven is filled with souls who cherish them as much as you do. Mothers, there will be children who divert from the heavenly path at times. You must try not to be alarmed because this is not uncommon. Pray constantly for these souls, of course, but show them peace in the face of their rebellion. Explain that they have left the heavenly path and that if they are off the path when Christ comes, there is the danger of not getting back to the path in time to get to Heaven. I speak of course about older children who have rejected Christ and Christian living. I hear the cries of mothers who worry over these rebellious ones. That is why I speak of it. Remember that Christ is all mercy to a mother. Your maternal prayers are powerful so continue to pray for your child, but do not think that all is lost, regardless of the circumstances. Even in the direst cases, Jesus will forgive all for the sake of a holy mother. So really, there is nothing you should upset yourself with, dear mothers. Our Lord will save your children and protect their eternities. Your job is to cooperate with Him. Speak the truth to your children fearlessly, in kindness and love, and they will belong to Christ.

June 11, 2004
Mary (an unknown saint) Speaks to Mothers

Mothers of this time have many fears and justifiably so. The world seeks to snatch souls from Jesus and attempts to entice children away from the path. Mothers, do not fear, but talk to your children about sin. When a child commits an act that is sinful, you must tell that child that he has committed a sin. You must then make a habit of participating in the Sacrament of Reconciliation so that the child understands that while he has committed a sin, there is forgiveness available. You must secure your children's habit now, so that when grown they understand not only that a sin has been committed, but how they should go about cleansing their soul. They must know that they have a need for this sacrament so always point this out to them. Mothers, be certain your children participate in this sacrament often. These habits stick, which is why it is so important to ingrain them in souls when they are young. If you do this, you will see your children taking responsibility for their mistakes as adults. This is what the world is lacking during this time of darkness. There is a great deal of blame being laid by souls who refuse to acknowledge that they make mistakes. In this way, they do not have to change sinful patterns of behavior. The world reinforces this by the constant game of blaming someone or something other than the person who committed the act. Mothers, do not allow this to happen in your home. Be kind and understanding always, but if a child commits an act that has risen to the level of sinful behavior, you have an obligation to call it by name and the name of such an act is sin. It can be difficult if your husband is not following the same path. This is a great cross for you and also a great cross for your children. In that case you must pray with the greatest of diligence, every day, for your husband's conversion. You must also continue to set the example, often in the face of ridicule, that you will not be enticed to sin simply because your husband is behaving in a rebellious way. Many marriages today are ill advised because one of the parties has no intention of following Christ. If this is the case, you must not marry this person. You cannot be expected to bring up children as Christians if your husband refuses to acknowledge Christ as the Leader. Take heart, though, if you are in this situation. Do your best, dear woman, and let Jesus flow into your home with special graces. He will do this and He will hear your pleas for peace in your home. And do not lose hope that your husband will convert. Your children will also know the truth, and, although there will be times when it suits them to follow the path of the non-believer, they will return to Christ. The best way, indeed the only way, to have a holy family is to live in holiness and allow Christ to protect your family. He will do this for you.

June 12, 2004
Mary (an unknown saint) Speaks to Mothers

We must all give great thanks and praise to God the Father for allowing these many graces to flow down into your world. It is a sign of His great mercy that so many of us are allowed to speak to you. I have a special bond with mothers, of course, because so much of my life was spent in this role. I want to say a brief word to mothers of children who are ill or who struggle with disability. Mothers, your little child will be perfectly healed in Heaven. You must believe that God understands your heartache and that He wishes to walk with you in this heartache at each moment. I know how difficult this may be, but try to accept that God had a purpose for allowing your child to experience this suffering. You are a part of that purpose so be certain that you continually ask God to send each and every grace available to you. Set a tone of joyful acceptance always and your child will understand that he is precious and perfect in your eyes and in the eyes of God. I lost a little child to sickness so I understand the great sorrow attached to this heavy cross. You will never regret that you accepted great sorrow for Christ. Believe me please when I tell you that in Heaven all is joy. If you are struggling with crosses involving your children, you must cry out often to Heaven, sometimes all day long. Heaven will help you in many ways, but the most important grace that Heaven will send is peace, and peace will soothe your family and decrease the weight of your cross. Do not compare your family life to others, who live only for the world. You must live for Heaven and for the Kingdom, so compare your family life to that of the Holy Family. Jesus, Mary, and Joseph lived simply and humbly, offering all to Heaven. They often went quietly without for lack of money. They spent time in exile. They served God in everything, seeking only His will. They were fair and just in their dealings with others and used the family home setting to increase their virtues by selfless service to each other. Mary, our Heavenly Mother, is the model of all mothers. She was kind, gentle, and she was constant and consistent. She did not require long holidays from her role as mother. Her husband and Child were her first priority and her role in her home was her vocation. Joseph is the model for fathers and wishes to speak with you himself. In Heaven, Joseph is honored with the greatest of reverence. His faith alone makes him worthy of the greatest reward, but his humility also bears mention. He will speak to all, but especially to fathers. I thank God for allowing me, Mary, a humble little saint in Heaven's ranks, to speak with you. Call on me for anything. My love and prayers are with you.

Part Two:
St. Joseph
Speaks to Fathers

June 14, 2004
St. Joseph Speaks to Fathers

I send the most affectionate greetings to my brothers and sisters on earth. I have come particularly to speak to fathers during this time of darkness. If you have been given a child or the care of a child, you must take responsibility for the formation and support of that child. I wish to share a glimpse of my family with you, so that you can follow the example we have set. There were three of us, Jesus, Mary, and me, Joseph. I took responsibility, as much as possible, for the support of the family. We were poor, it is true, because we lived in difficult times and for a time we were exiled. When you move to a land that is not your home, you are at a disadvantage, often, with regard to work. That was the case with me, and while I was skilled at my profession, I found it difficult to obtain as much work as I would have liked. Nevertheless, I made enough to keep us and we lived simply. I taught my Son that work was to be enjoyed and that through work a soul gave God great glory. I worked steadily and thoroughly, always being scrupulously honest and fair. My reputation was sound and I would have been known as a just man, both professionally and personally. I understood that my responsibility to Jesus was important to the Kingdom. I had the task of accompanying Him through His precious childhood. Jesus, I must say, did not require any real correcting, because He was a most beautiful and sweet boy. His kindness brought tears to my eyes, sometimes many times in one day. I will say truly that He was an example to me. With that said, however, I also tried to be an example to Him and so must you be to your children. While I understand that you are not called upon to accompany Jesus through His childhood, you must understand that your child or children are equally precious in their humanity, because each little soul is of equal value in the Kingdom. Each day and each moment of each day is an opportunity to teach your child what it is to be a follower in God's Kingdom.

If I were allowed, I could write pages and pages, speaking only of the holiness of Mary, the Mother of Christ. Can you imagine the honor that was mine? I was given the task of parenting with Mary as my partner. I will say briefly that Mary was the kindest, most gentle and most humble woman ever created by God. You must not think that she was given these virtues or that it was easy for her. This was not the case. Mary sacrificed each day and practiced these virtues. She was another constant source of example to me. How could I have been anything but virtuous living with these two heavenly creatures? Fathers, mine is the honor of instructing you on leading your families to Christ. Thank our loving Father in

Heaven for this grace because it is a very beautiful thing for Him to allow. Treat these words with humility and reverence and He, the God of All, will bring peace and joy to your families. You can be another pocket of holiness, as we were, and I will show you how. Remember that you have great and limitless help in Heaven. Do not be discouraged if your family is struggling with worldly influences at this moment. I will help you and together we will move toward the example that our little Holy Family has set for you. All is well. Let us begin.

June 15, 2004
St. Joseph Speaks to Fathers

Fathers of the world, listen carefully to my words. Please understand that you will be held accountable for your parenting. In most cases, a father should be with his children. In cases where he cannot, through circumstances beyond his control, that is different. But I speak to the majority of fathers at this time. Your children are your treasure and they are also a large part of your salvation. You will gain the greatest of graces through your parenting of your children. To begin with the most fundamental advice, you must be with your children in order to properly parent them. Many fathers today view the role of father simply as a provider. They feel that as long as they are providing for their children's material needs, their job has been completed. Fathers, you know this is not the case. Providing for your children's material needs is only one aspect of your role as father. You must accept that if you are not at work, generally speaking, you should be with your family. Children learn from observing and modeling. They cannot do this if you are not in their company. Be with your children, fathers. You need do nothing, only set a calm example. Be about your household chores and let the children see that you are dutiful. Another current trend that concerns Heaven is that of purity. Fathers, children must learn how important it is to be pure. Are your children learning this from you? They will learn it by observing the entertainment you participate in. How do you respond to television shows that depict impure actions and situations? Fathers, these things are not acceptable for you. You must not watch television programs that illustrate mortal sin. Certainly your children should not watch these things either. That, dear men, is a profound truth, and if you are allowing your children to view behaviors on television that depict sin, you are in effect teaching them these behaviors. You must understand that by not objecting to these things, you are teaching your children that these behaviors are acceptable. This must stop. When you reject a program because it is illustrating unChristian-like behaviors, you must take the opportunity to explain to your children why you are doing so and why the behavior you rejected is not Christian. Do you understand? You must ask me to help you in this issue if you are unsure because homes are being contaminated constantly in this manner. This form of entertainment is unsuitable for you, dear men of God. You want to come to Heaven, do you not? Then you must begin to prepare yourselves on earth. You can do this by spending time with your children in purity, and doing things together that do not offend God. You will be accountable for each word you say to your children. God does not expect you to be perfect. Do not be afraid. You will make mistakes, of course, and that is understood and forgiven. But you must not allow a pattern of entertainment in your home that is objectionable to Heaven. Consider always what Jesus would say about an entertainment. He is with you, you know, at each moment. Be aware of His presence and you can then judge your actions and activities by His standard. I will help you to escape from any bad habits that have taken hold of you. Be cheerful and courageous and together we will purify your life.

June 16, 2004
St. Joseph Speaks to Fathers

Dear fathers of the world, you must heed my voice. I am speaking to you from kindness and concern. We in Heaven watch the events in the world because we are eager to assist you. We hear your prayers and immediately begin interceding for you so that any graces available will be utilized. Allow us to help you to examine your role as father so you can be certain you are fulfilling this role as God has willed. You must examine your role in comparison to me, Joseph, the head of the Holy Family. Do not examine your role in comparison to a soul who is not following God. You must take this opportunity to also look at your companions. Are they true followers? Do they encourage you to be a good father and husband? Are they themselves good fathers and husbands? Dear man, if they are not fulfilling their role as father and husband, it will be difficult for you to resist their influence. Many in this time will encourage you to put yourself first, but I tell you in all seriousness that you should not do this. Your wife and children must come first. You are to lead your family to Heaven. In Heaven, the first will be last. Consider yourself a servant to your family. In this way you will not spend too much time meditating on how you would like to follow the world. You live in a world of great darkness. I must speak the truth so that you know that it is critical that your family be steered safely through these times. With the help of Heaven, you will do this successfully. But in order to obtain this help, you must ask for it. In order to ask for it, you must be prayerful. If you are not prayerful, you will not see the need to pray because you will be too busy scurrying from one day to the next and telling yourself that all is well because this is what everyone else is doing. Fathers, set a tone of quietness in your home whenever possible. Children in your care will then feel free to come to you with their little difficulties and fears. Be available to them by often sitting quietly or working in silence. There is no need for the constant distraction of noise. It dulls your soul, dear man, and God cannot find rest in you. If you spend time in quietness, your soul will calm and your God can claim you and communicate with you. He will inspire you to give consideration to His will for your life. He will give you an awareness of the large view of your life and your family, pulling you away from the small view, which is the moment. If your large view includes Heaven and serving God, you will understand that you must live each moment differently. Set your sight on Heaven, for both you and your family, and you will see your perspective begin to shift a little here and alter a little there. This is a process and you can be comfortable that all will not change in a day, *particularly if you have been spending too much time in the world or practicing bad habits. But it will change. Gradually, your home will feel different to you. You will long for holiness for each of the souls in your family who are walking your life journey with you. You will see their spiritual development as the priority. Dearest man, created by God, this is your role. You, in partnership with your wife, are to shepherd your little ones through their childhoods so that they can grow strong in the service to the Kingdom. Be brave and allow me, Joseph, to show you how this should be done.*

June 17, 2004
St. Joseph Speaks to Fathers

Dear sons of God, you must treat fatherhood like the great honor that it is. By allowing you to provide formation to a child, our God has placed a degree of trust in you. You will not want to disappoint Him. You must listen to Him for direction on what your children require for the best possible preparation in life. Because each soul is unique, the same approach that works for one will not work for all. Each child will need thoughtful consideration given to the approach that will best suit his or her nature. Fathers, when do you give the rearing of your children this consideration? You should spend some time each day thinking of your children and what they need. It is important, of course, that they be fed and clothed, but not to excess. It is important that they have shelter and, if possible, an education. What I want to stress to you, fathers of the world, is that your children need your love, along with these other things. Children, more than anything, must know that their father loves them and considers them precious. Your actions every day will tell your children how you feel about them. If you are called on to correct a child, do so gently, with love. If a child angers you, you must remember that you were once a child and made similar mistakes. Do not frighten your children, fathers. This is not love. This is the opposite of love. Your child should respect you, of course, and you should not tolerate behavior that will not be welcome in the Kingdom, but expect some bad behavior and expect to have to gently correct your children. Fathers often make the mistake of thinking that their primary function with children is that of disciplinarian. This is an error. Your primary function as a father is to love and then to set an example that your children can follow which will result in eternity in Heaven. Are you doing this, dear man? Be vigilant in examining your own behavior and be certain that your children are not mimicking something in you when they misbehave. This is important, so pay heed. I love you dearly, men of the world. I understand the influences with which you struggle. That is why you must spend time in prayer, and not with entertainment. Your Jesus wants to help you and He wants you to help Him. This is a dark time for mankind because many have said "no" to God and to holy living. If you have done this, you must tell Jesus today that you are willing to change and that you desire that He help you. I tell you most sincerely that Jesus will handle everything if you are willing to change. He will forgive you every sin. He will mitigate any damage that neglect has done to your children. Jesus, in short, will solve your problems but you must spend time in silence with Him. Make prayer the most important part of your day, fathers. Only in this way can you determine what Jesus requires from you with regard to your life and your parenting. Heaven understands that you have pressures and that you must earn your living and support your family. Heaven respects these things because it is Heaven who has ordained this way of life for you. You must constantly ask Heaven to guide you in these matters, as well as in spiritual matters. We will hear your prayers and assist you. But you must be the head of your family now and set a tone of respect for God.

June 18, 2004
St. Joseph Speaks to Fathers

Again today I call out to fathers. Dear men, you must face your mistakes fearlessly. Examine with me the way that you live. Do you live for God? If God were to call you home to Heaven today, could you lie down peacefully, content that you had worthily accepted your vocation as husband and father? As human beings, created by God, we are all subject to His time. When He decrees that your time on earth has passed, it has passed. There will be no second chances with regard to either your life or your parenting. When your children are grown, the opportunity to influence them diminishes. You should never give up setting an example for your children and attempting to help them to see the straight path to Heaven, but you can do far more with children than adults. So you see, dear man, that you must seize the opportunity to mold your child when he is small. Many souls on earth think that they are entitled to great amounts of relaxation and play time. I tell you most solemnly that play time is for children. If you are an adult, you should be concerned with serving Christ, and not with entertaining yourself. If you spend time in silent prayer, considering Jesus and what He did for you, you will understand what it is He asks that you do for Him. This is simple, I know, but I assure you that few men are giving

Christ this time to work in their souls. It is for this reason we have reached the current level of darkness. Historically man said "no" to sin. In this day man says "yes" to sin. Children suffer because if man is saying "yes" to sin, he is saying "no" to his vocation. You cannot live two ways, my dear friend, so you must make a choice. Choose God. There is no future for you or your family in choosing darkness. Do not underestimate the power of God to assist a soul who seeks goodness. He will help you.

I would like to speak about how I treated Mary, my wife on earth. I treated her with the greatest dignity and respect. I tried to help her when I could, and I remained in constant awareness of her comfort and happiness. I was unable to provide her with great wealth, and sometimes we were forced to go without, subsisting on the barest of necessities. She did not complain and I did not rail against God for placing us in trying times. I humbly placed my little family in the care of God and did the best I could to provide for them. Dear men of the world, there are those who are in far more need than you, whatever your circumstances. You must be content with what God has given you. Remember that there will always be those with more, and there will always be those with less. Praise God in everything and you will be cared for by Heaven. When you worry about material things, consider what would happen if you were to do without many of the things you have today. Would you starve? Spend some time considering what it is your body needs for survival and I think you will see that you have been given these things. There may come a time when you do not have as much as you have today. How you will shake your heads at your former complaints. Do you understand what I am trying to tell you? Do not wish for more; wish to be happier with less. Pray this way and God will help you by showing you that you do not need all of these things with which you surround yourself. These things are a distraction. Your families are no happier than those who have less, and this I say from experience. We were very happy on earth and we had little. Keep a heavenly perspective and you will not feel that you require more.

June 19, 2004
St. Joseph Speaks to Fathers

Dear men, destined to serve God, please consider that your first duty is to your family. Indeed, caring for your wife and children is your sacred duty, and all of Heaven will help you to make this your priority. God's love will flow through you into your home, and He, through you, will be the leader of your family. Do you want this to happen? Look closely at your home and family and determine if it is already this way. If it is, then all is well and we will continue on, Heaven working closely with you to steer your family through difficult times. If this is not the case, then you must understand that there is work to be done in your life. Most men in today's world have a little work to do, so do not be discouraged if you see things that must be removed from your life. Be brave and steady and you will come to know God's will for you. Dear man, you were created by God to serve during this time and God needs your service. He is calling out to all of His children now and asking that souls put aside worldly desires in favor of heavenly desires. Come to the most direct path to Heaven and do not leave this path again. Please. In a very short time, you will be so glad that you served. These times are not ordinary times, my dear friend. These are extraordinary times and the greatest of heavenly help is available for God's servants.

Do not be anxious by this. Be grateful. Jesus is all good. If you but knew the depth of His compassion and love for you, there would be no need for any words at all. But souls in the world have been distracted and the view to Heaven has been all but obliterated by the darkness of sin. There is little joy on earth and many souls wander in despair. You must not do that. You are a child of the Kingdom and you must walk in joy. I will show you the path to joy. As a man of God, you have the greatest of dignity as your right. That dignity comes from living a purposeful life in union with Jesus. When you seek His will, look no further than your family and you will find your path to salvation. Join us, the army that seeks to wage war on darkness. We are brave and loyal to our King. Our King, Jesus Christ, gives us all that we require for this battle. He has a particular mission for you but you must sit in silence and ask Him to reveal it to you. I, Joseph, am very close to the Savior. I will intercede for you to help you eradicate sin in your life and restore your heavenly role to its rightful level of holiness. Be at peace in everything, but do not hesitate to answer "yes" to God.

Part Three:
Jesus Speaks to Children

August 2, 2004
Jesus

My servants must remember that sin is an intentional mistake and should not be confused with an unintentional mistake, such as dropping a glass. Little children very often obey their impulses and commit small transgressions, such as striking out at another. Along with our Blessed Mother, Mary, I refer to these acts as mistakes. This is acceptable when referring to the acts of children. Deliberate acts of malice, committed by older children or adults, should be referred to as sin, which is always forgivable.

Prayers for Children

- Jesus, forgive them.

- Mother Mary, help me to be good.

- God in Heaven, You are the Creator of all things. Please send Your graces down upon our world.

- Jesus, I love You.

- Jesus, I offer You my day.

June 21, 2004
Jesus Speaks to Children

Dear children of the world, how I love you. You were created by God the Father and He created each one of you with the most careful thought. Indeed, in Heaven's eyes, you are perfect. I am Jesus, and I am in Heaven with the Father. But because I am God and come from God, I can do anything. I am powerful, dear children, but I do not like to show off, so I do not use My powers in silly ways. I use My powers in important ways, that will help people. One way that I use My power is to make people happy when they are sad or worried. Are you sad or worried? If you are, then you must come to Me and I will make you happy again. It is important for you to know how to come to Me so I am going to tell you. When you wish to come to Me, Jesus, and tell Me about your problems, you must pray. There are many ways to pray and they are all perfect. One way to pray is to close your eyes and speak to Me silently in your head. You might wonder how I can hear you if you are speaking silently. That is part of My magic, dear little child. When you wish to speak to Me, your Jesus, who is your very best friend, you can speak to Me at any time, in any place. I will hear you. I will listen carefully to your worries or to your trouble, and I will help you. You will not see Me, but I will be there. I am in Heaven, yes, as I told you. But I am also everywhere on the earth. Wherever you are, I am also. So if you are playing, I am there. If you are eating, I am there. If you are going to sleep at night, I am with you. You will never be in a place where I am not. I am your invisible friend and I never go away from you. So tell Me everything that worries you, because I love you and I want to know. I can help you with many problems. You will know that I am with you because after you speak to Me you will feel a bit better. That is My magic. You must trust Me in everything because I love you very much. I think you are perfect. I am going to tell you about Me so that you know you have a very powerful invisible friend.

June 22, 2004
Jesus Speaks to Children

I am with you, dear children of the world. I am with you everywhere. Do not be afraid because I am all powerful and I am your friend. You understand that when you are finished in this world, you will come to My home, and that My home is in Heaven. I have prepared a beautiful place for you to live, where you will be very happy with all of the people you love from earth. Heaven is the nicest place you could ever imagine. There are beautiful lakes and streams where you can play. You will never be hungry or afraid in Heaven because there is no badness. No one can hurt you in Heaven. You will have many friends here and you will never be sick. Heaven is the perfect place and it is filled with My friends because I am Jesus and I am God. Do you want to come to Heaven? You are welcome here, My dearest child, because I love you. I will be waiting for you and when you are finished on earth, I will take you to Heaven. What a happy day that will be! You will be happy because you are coming to this wonderful place, and I will be happy because I am going to be with you forever. Everyone in Heaven will be happy because they love you already and wait for you to come here to join them. They have so much to show you and to tell you. You will have great fun in Heaven, little child. Sometimes, when you are sad or afraid on earth, you might say, "Jesus, come and take me to Heaven now." But I cannot do that, dearest child of My heart, until it is time. You have to finish your time on earth first. I am the only one who knows when your life is finished and it is My job to come for you. Do not worry, though, because I will come for you the very moment you are finished with your work. You see, My friends who are here with Me in Heaven helped Me while they were on earth. I am your Jesus and I need help from all of My friends now. Soon I will tell you about your job so that you will know how you can help Me, too.

June 23, 2004
Jesus Speaks to Children

I have told you about Heaven. You will be happy here and this is truly your home. Now I want to tell you how you can help Me. I am part of a family and so are you. We are part of the same family. It is a bigger family than you belong to on earth. This bigger family includes all people. I want all people to come home to Heaven when they are finished on earth but some will need help because they are not trying hard enough to be good. Are you trying to be good? Well, this is the first way that I need your help. I, your Jesus, am asking you to try to be good. When you try to be good, it is like you are giving Me a present. Would you like to give your Jesus a present? Just do your best to be a good boy or a good girl and you will make Me very happy. I can use your present and turn it into forgiveness for someone who is making mistakes. You will make mistakes too sometimes, so you understand that it can be hard to be good. But I forgive you every mistake that you have made and I will forgive you every mistake that you will ever make. I would like to forgive everyone for their mistakes but some people do not want to say they are sorry. You see, My little friend, all a soul needs to do to come to Heaven, is to try to be good and then to say they are sorry when they make a mistake. Even if they have made many terrible mistakes, I forgive them. But they have to say they are sorry, just like you say you are sorry when you hurt someone. Trying to be good while you are on earth is like doing your job for your heavenly family. I will tell you now another way that you can help Me. You must say often, "Jesus, forgive them." You do not need to say it out loud if you do not want to. You can say it in your head because remember that I told you I can hear you speaking even when you are speaking silently. If you say this, "Jesus, forgive them," I can save many people and bring them to Heaven. I want everyone in Heaven so this will be helping Me. Will you do that for Me? You are My friend and I am your friend. I will give you a big reward for helping Me and I will give you many presents when you come to Heaven. Thank you, dear friend. I am your Jesus and I thank you.

June 24, 2004
Jesus Speaks to Children

Dear children of the world, I am happy to be talking with you. You are so precious to Me and I think of you all day, every day. I watch you when you are unhappy and I hope that you will talk to Me so that I can make you feel better. I will always be close to you so you can talk to Me whenever you wish. The most important thing for you to remember is that I am with you. There are two other important things for you to remember also. One is that I love everyone, even when they are making mistakes. Do not think that I stop loving a person because they do the wrong thing. I love them just as much and I love you just as much when you do the wrong thing. The second thing you must remember is that you can talk to Me when you make a mistake. Come to Me quickly when you do something wrong. If you come to Me, I can make you feel better and forgive you at once. In that way you will not feel sad inside and make more mistakes because you feel badly. That can happen, with adults as well as children. So you must remember that your Jesus loves you always, even when you make mistakes. And you must also remember that if you make a mistake, you must talk to Me right away. Tell Me about the mistake and say you are sorry. I will then help you not to make more mistakes. You see, My beautiful child, I can help you with everything. You must ask Me to help you and you can be certain that I will.

June 25, 2004
Jesus Speaks to Children

My dearest children, I want you to know Me. I know you perfectly. I know what makes you happy and I know what frightens you. I am your Jesus and I am your God. You hear many stories about kings. Well, I am the greatest King because I am the King of all people. Most stories that you hear are pretend stories, about imaginary kings. Dear child, I am real. My story is a true story and you can believe everything that I tell you. I am truly with you. I will never leave you. And at the end of your life I will come for you to bring you to Heaven. Be happy, little one. Your Jesus loves you most tenderly. I want to tell you today about the different parts of you. You have two parts. You have a body and you have a soul. Your body carries your soul because your soul is inside your body. The body, your arms and legs and everything else, is the part you can see. The soul is the invisible part. You cannot see it, like you cannot see Me, but it is there. Your soul is beautiful and I am in your soul. You must always try to eat so that your body can feel good and grow. Well, it is the very same with your soul. You must always try to pray because that is how you feed your soul. Whenever you talk to Me in prayer, your soul becomes stronger and grows. If you never talk to Me, your soul might feel sick or weak. How will you know if your soul is sick? I will tell you. You will know if your soul is sick because you will begin to feel unhappy. I do not want you to be unhappy. There are many people who have very sick bodies but they are happy and that is because they have a very healthy soul. When you die in your body, as everyone does, it is time for your soul to live and so your soul comes to Heaven with Me. It is your soul that I will come to collect at the end of your life. During your time on earth, when you will live in your body, you must always remember to feed your soul so that it is nice and strong because a nice strong soul will get you straight to Heaven. Talk to Me often, dear child. Talking to Me is prayer and it is prayer that makes your soul grow strong.

June 26, 2004
Jesus Speaks to Children

My little ones, it is My greatest wish that you remain close to Me. I do not want you to live your life thinking that Jesus is not with you and that Jesus does not love you. Always remember Me and remember that I love you. I will help you, dear child. I will help you in many ways. Sometimes you might be with people who do not love Me. You must pray for them. Ask Me to help them and I will do so. You have a great deal of power if you are My friend because you can ask Me to do things for you and I will, as long as you are asking Me to help others. Believe in Me, dear child. It hurts My feelings that so few believe in Me or talk to Me. Some people would rather have a lot of things than be My friend. I know that you love to have toys. I like you to have toys, too, because it is good for you to play. But I do not like you to have too many toys and I do not like you to keep your toys all for yourself, never letting anyone else play. Share your toys and I will be happy. If you do not have a lot of toys, be happy, little child. You will have as much as you want in Heaven. You will have everything in Heaven that you wish for. It is often better if you do not have a lot of things on earth because then you are not tempted to become selfish or greedy. People are selfish and greedy when they want to have many things and keep them all to themselves. I have given you the world where you live. I gave you clouds, sunshine, water, trees, and grass. All of these things come from Me because I created all of these things. Every so often you should try to give something away and pretend that you are giving it to Me. If you give anything away, dearest child, I will give you credit for giving it to Me and I will give you back far more when you reach Heaven. Always share. It is good for you and makes Me very happy. I love you perfectly. I will always love you perfectly. I am your friend. I am Jesus.

Part Four:
Mary, our Blessed Mother, Speaks to Children

June 29, 2004
Mary, our Blessed Mother, Speaks to Children

Dearest little children, I am Mary, your Heavenly Mother. I am the Mother of Jesus and the Mother of all people also. I want to tell you about Jesus because it is so important that you know about Him. You see, my dearest little children, Jesus loves you very much. He wants to bring each one of you safely to Heaven. Heaven is your real home, where you will live forever. Many souls on earth forget about Heaven and think that earth is their only home. This is not true and if you believe that earth is your only home, you will not try to earn Heaven and you will make many mistakes. If you always think about Heaven, and being good so that you can get to Heaven, you will do better and Jesus will be happy. I am your Heavenly Mother and I help many souls get to Heaven. You can talk to me as well as to Jesus. I will help you with many things, but mostly I will help you learn about Jesus and learn how to love Him. I am His helper, you see, so my job is to bring souls to Him. I will do that for you if you would like me to. You can say simply, "Mother, help me to be good." I will hear you immediately and I will begin helping you. In this way you will have someone who loves you and understands you and who is always looking out for you. Call on me often, my beautiful little child, because I am your Heavenly Mother and I love you.

June 29, 2004
Mary, our Blessed Mother, Speaks to Children

How happy I am to be talking to you in this way! God is very good to allow me to do so. You see, dear children, usually God does not allow people in Heaven to communicate with people on earth. God is allowing it now because this is a special time. During this time, your time on earth, Heaven is doing special work. There are many souls on earth who do not understand that God is the One who is in charge of everything. These people think they are in charge and they are trying to be better than God. This is a mistake for them and they must change. All people must understand that God created the world and each person in the world. God allows the sun to shine, God allows the rain to fall. If God did not allow these things to happen, these things would stop. We must always thank God for making the world so beautiful for us. When you thank God for making the world and making you, He is happy and He sends even more graces down to the world. Graces are good things that come from Heaven. So you must join me, Mary, your Mother in Heaven, and ask God for more graces from Heaven for the world. Will you do that? Will you help me? Together we will say, "God in Heaven, You are the Creator of all things. Please send Your graces down upon our world." I thank you, dear children. I love you very much. I will help you in everything. Like Jesus, I can always hear you, so talk to me often. I will always be close to you.

June 30, 2004
Mary, our Blessed Mother, Speaks to Children

Dear little children of Heaven, your Blessed Mother loves you. I look with such happiness on you as you play and work. All of Heaven watches you and helps you when you are in trouble. Be happy knowing this. Be happy in the thought that Jesus also loves you and watches you with delight. You are Heaven's little treasures and your prayers are so important to us here. When a child speaks to Heaven, God the Father always listens carefully because children pray the most favorable prayers. Your prayers are often even more powerful than an adult's prayers because usually children are more pure. Being pure is important, little children. Do not use bad words or watch bad things on television because if you do these things, your purity will go away. Purity means always trying to think about good and happy things. Think about me, your Heavenly Mother, and Jesus, your Heavenly King. Think about all of the wonderful saints in Heaven. Saints are people who lived in the world and did a good job for Jesus. You can be a saint, too, and that is what I want for you. I want you to be my little saint. Will you try to do that for me? I will help you by reminding you when you should pray. When you think of me, say a prayer. When you think of Jesus, say a prayer. It does not have to be a big prayer. It can be simply, "Jesus, I love

You." That is a good prayer to say and it will make Jesus and me so happy. I am with you, little child of my heart. I am always with you.

July 1, 2004
Mary, our Blessed Mother,
Speaks to Children

Dearest little children, I am your Heavenly Mother and I love you. I want to bring you to Jesus. I do that by helping you to understand the great love Jesus has for you. Many souls think of God as someone far away who is very busy with the business of Heaven. This is not true. Jesus is God and Jesus is very busy looking after souls on earth. Jesus loves you most tenderly. Jesus loves you so much that He died on the cross for you. He died on the cross so that Heaven's doors would be open to every boy and girl in the world. And Heaven's doors are open to you, little child. We wait for you to come to Heaven so that you will be happy forever. I want you to know that each soul makes mistakes on earth. That is why Jesus chose to die for you. He knew you would make mistakes. He wanted to be certain that there was enough forgiveness for each mistake made by every person. Never worry about your mistakes. Even the greatest saints made many mistakes. You say you are sorry to Jesus and Jesus forgives you for your mistake and He forgets about your mistake. Sometimes children think that they are bad because they have made mistakes and this is simply not true. I am your Heavenly Mother and I look into your little heart and I see such goodness. You can do great things for Jesus if you try to do your best. Will

71

you do that for me? Try to be good and all will be well.

July 2, 2004
Mary, our Blessed Mother, Speaks to Children

Dearest children, you must live for your Jesus. When you awaken in the morning you should tell Jesus you love Him and say, "Jesus, I offer You my day." Little children, if you do this, then Jesus will take every part of your work and play, your eating and sleeping, and He will use it to bring other souls to Heaven. Isn't that easy? You see, my little ones, it is not hard to please Jesus. He is loving and happy and wants you to be loving and happy. If you do as I say, you will be happy because it is in being good that we become happy. You must never worry if someone is not good. Just pray for them and we will help them. You may not see us helping them but you can believe that we will because I would never tell you something that was not true. Neither would Jesus. We speak only the truth. You should practice speaking only the truth, also. You may make some small mistakes at times and at times you may forget to pray. Simply tell Jesus you forgot and pray a small prayer. All will be well. If you practice these little things they will become good habits and you will become a beautiful little saint for Heaven. It is easier than you think, my precious ones. I am with you and I will help you with everything.

July 3, 2004
Mary, our Blessed Mother, Speaks to Children

My dearest children, I am glad to see that you have listened so carefully to the words we have sent you from Heaven. Now you know how to be good and how to please Jesus. Jesus, because He is God, knows everything and He knows exactly what is best for you. At times you may pray and you may feel that your prayer was not answered. My dearest little child, Jesus made the world for you. Do not think He would not give you everything in that world. But sometimes, because Jesus knows everything, He knows that you may be asking for something that would be bad for you. In this case, Jesus must say "no." You understand, don't you? Perhaps you are asking for a red car but you are too small to drive. Jesus will say "no" to that prayer. I want you to know that Jesus is the smartest and most clever man who ever lived. He sees everything and knows everything, because He is God. His decisions are always the right decisions so you can trust Him in everything. I want to tell you another way you can please Jesus. You must tell Him this: "Jesus, I trust in You. Jesus, I trust in You. Jesus, I trust in You." If you say that three times, it is a most beautiful prayer and you will then begin to trust Him in everything, which will make you feel safe and happy. I love you dearly, my little child. I place my hands over you in a protective blessing. Try to be good and I will help you.

Appendix

The Lay Apostolate of
Jesus Christ the Returning King

We seek to be united to Jesus in our daily work, and through our vocations, in order to obtain graces for the conversion of sinners. Through our cooperation with the Holy Spirit, we will allow Jesus to flow through us to the world, bringing His light. We do this in union with Mary, our Blessed Mother, with the Communion of Saints, with all of God's holy angels, and with our fellow lay apostles in the world.

Guidelines for Lay Apostles

As lay apostles of Jesus Christ the Returning King, we agree to perform our basic obligations as practicing Catholics. Additionally, we will adopt the following spiritual practices, as best we can:

1. **Allegiance Prayer** and **Morning Offering**, plus a brief prayer for the Holy Father
2. **Eucharistic Adoration**, one hour per week
3. **Prayer Group Participation**, monthly, at which we pray the Luminous Mysteries of the Holy Rosary and read the Monthly Message
4. **Monthly Confession**
5. Further, we will follow the example of Jesus Christ as set out in the Holy Scripture, treating all others with His patience and kindness.

Allegiance Prayer

Dear God in Heaven, I pledge my allegiance to You. I give You my life, my work and my heart. In turn, give me the grace of obeying Your every direction to the fullest possible extent. Amen.

Morning Offering

O Jesus, through the Immaculate Heart of Mary, I offer You the prayers, works, joys and sufferings of this day, for all the intentions of Your Sacred Heart, in union with the Holy Sacrifice of the Mass throughout the world, in reparation for my sins, and for the intentions of the Holy Father. Amen.

Prayer for the Holy Father

Blessed Mother of Jesus, protect our Holy Father, Benedict XVI, and bless his intentions.

Five Luminous Mysteries

1. The Baptism of Jesus
2. The Wedding at Cana
3. The Proclamation of the Kingdom of God
4. The Transfiguration
5. The Institution of the Eucharist

Promise from Jesus to His Lay Apostles

May 12, 2005

Your message to souls remains constant. Welcome each soul to the rescue mission. You may assure each lay apostle that just as they concern themselves with My interests, I will concern Myself with theirs. They will be placed in My Sacred Heart and I will defend and protect them. I will also pursue complete conversion of each of their loved ones. So you see, the souls who serve in this rescue mission as My beloved lay apostles will know peace. The world cannot make this promise as only Heaven can bestow peace on a soul. This is truly Heaven's mission and I call every one of Heaven's children to assist Me. You will be well rewarded, My dear ones.

Prayers taken from The Volumes

Prayers to God the Father

"What can I do for my Father in Heaven?"

"I trust You, God. I offer You my pain in the spirit of acceptance and I will serve You in every circumstance."

"God my Father in Heaven, You are all mercy. You love me and see my every sin. God, I call on You now as the Merciful Father. Forgive my every sin. Wash away the stains on my soul so that I may once again rest in complete innocence. I trust You, Father in Heaven. I rely on You. I thank You. Amen."

"God my Father, calm my spirit and direct my path."

"God, I have made mistakes. I am sorry. I am Your child, though, and seek to be united to You."

"I believe in God. I believe Jesus is calling me. I believe my Blessed Mother has requested my help. Therefore I am going to pray on this day and every day."

"God my Father, help me to understand."

Prayers to Jesus

"Jesus, I give You my day."

"Jesus, how do You want to use me on this day? You have a willing servant in me, Jesus. Allow me to work for the Kingdom."

"Lord, what can I do today to prepare for Your coming? Direct me, Lord, and I will see to Your wishes."

"Lord, help me."

"Jesus, love me."

Prayers to the Angels

"Angels from Heaven, direct my path."

"Dearest angel guardian, I desire to serve Jesus by remaining at peace. Please obtain for me the graces necessary to maintain His divine peace in my heart."

Prayers for a Struggling Soul

"Jesus, what do You think of all this? Jesus, what do You want me to do for this soul? Jesus, show me how to bring You into this situation."

"Angel guardian, thank you for your constant vigil over this soul. Saints in Heaven, please assist this dear angel."

Prayers for Children

"God in Heaven, You are the Creator of all things. Please send Your graces down upon our world."

"Jesus, I love You."

"Jesus, I trust in You. Jesus, I trust in You. Jesus, I trust in You."

"Jesus, I offer You my day."

"Mother Mary, help me to be good."

How to Recite the Chaplet of Divine Mercy

The Chaplet of Mercy is recited using ordinary Rosary beads of five decades. The Chaplet is preceded by two opening prayers from the *Diary* of Saint Faustina and followed by a closing prayer.

1. Make the Sign of the Cross

In the name of the Father, and of the Son, and of the Holy Spirit. Amen.

2. Optional Opening Prayers

You expired, Jesus, but the source of life gushed forth for souls, and the ocean of mercy opened up for the whole world. O Fount of Life, unfathomable Divine Mercy, envelop the whole world and empty Yourself out upon us.

O Blood and Water, which gushed forth from the Heart of Jesus as a fountain of mercy for us, I trust in You!

3. Our Father

Our Father, who art in Heaven, hallowed be Thy name. Thy Kingdom come. Thy will be done on earth as it is in Heaven. Give us this day our daily bread. And forgive us our trespasses, as we forgive those who trespass against us. And lead us not into temptation, but deliver us from evil. Amen.

4. Hail Mary

Hail Mary, full of grace, the Lord is with thee. Blessed art thou among women, and blessed is the fruit of thy womb, Jesus. Holy Mary, Mother of God, pray for us sinners, now and at the hour of our death. Amen.

5. The Apostles' Creed

I believe in God, the Father Almighty, Creator of Heaven and earth. I believe in Jesus Christ, His only Son, our Lord. He was conceived by the power of the Holy Spirit and born of the Virgin Mary. He suffered under Pontius Pilate, was crucified, died, and was buried. He descended to the dead. On the third day He rose again. He ascended into Heaven, and is seated at the right hand of the Father. He will come again to judge the living and the dead. I believe in the Holy Spirit, the holy Catholic Church, the Communion of Saints, the forgiveness of sins, the resurrection of the body, and life everlasting. Amen.

6. The Eternal Father

Eternal Father, I offer You the Body and Blood, Soul and Divinity of Your dearly beloved Son, our Lord, Jesus Christ, in atonement for our sins and those of the whole world.

7. On the Ten Small Beads of Each Decade

For the sake of His Sorrowful Passion, have mercy on us and on the whole world.

8. Repeat for the remaining decades

Saying the "Eternal Father" (6) on the "Our Father" bead and then 10 "For the sake of His Sorrowful Passion" (7) on the following "Hail Mary" beads.

9. Conclude with Holy God

Holy God, Holy Mighty One, Holy Immortal One, have mercy on us and on the whole world.

10. Optional Closing Prayer

Eternal God, in whom mercy is endless and the treasury of compassion inexhaustible, look kindly upon us and increase Your mercy in us, that in difficult moments we might not despair nor become despondent, but with great confidence submit ourselves to Your holy will, which is Love and Mercy itself.

To learn more about the image of The Divine Mercy, the Chaplet of Divine Mercy and the series of revelations given to St. Faustina Kowalska please contact:

Marians of the Immaculate Conception
Stockbridge, Massachusetts 01263
Telephone 800-462-7426
www.marian.org

How to Pray the Rosary

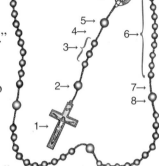

1. Make the Sign of the Cross and say the "Apostles Creed."
2. Say the "Our Father."
3. Say three "Hail Marys."
4. Say the "Glory be to the Father."
5. Announce the First Mystery; then say the "Our Father."
6. Say ten "Hail Marys," while meditating on the Mystery.
7. Say the "Glory be to the Father." After each decade say the following prayer requested by the Blessed Virgin Mary at Fatima: "O my Jesus, forgive us our sins, save us from the fires of hell, lead all souls to Heaven, especially those in most need of Thy mercy."
8. Announce the Second Mystery: then say the "Our Father." Repeat 6 and 7 and continue with the Third, Fourth, and Fifth Mysteries in the same manner.
9. Say the "Hail, Holy Queen" on the medal after the five decades are completed.

As a general rule, depending on the season, the Joyful Mysteries are said on Monday and Saturday; the Sorrowful Mysteries on Tuesday and Friday;

the Glorious Mysteries on Wednesday and Sunday; and the Luminous Mysteries on Thursday.

Papal Reflections of the Mysteries

The Joyful Mysteries

The Joyful Mysteries are marked by the joy radiating from the event of the Incarnation. This is clear from the very first mystery, the Annunciation, where Gabriel's greeting to the Virgin of Nazareth is linked to an invitation to messianic joy: "Rejoice, Mary." The whole of salvation... had led up to this greeting. (Prayed on Mondays and Saturdays, and optional on Sundays during Advent and the Christmas Season.)

The Luminous Mysteries

Moving on from the infancy and the hidden life in Nazareth to the public life of Jesus, our contemplation brings us to those mysteries which may be called in a special way "Mysteries of Light." Certainly, the whole mystery of Christ is a mystery of light. He is the "Light of the world" (John 8:12). Yet this truth emerges in a special way during the years of His public life. (Prayed on Thursdays.)

The Sorrowful Mysteries

The Gospels give great prominence to the Sorrowful Mysteries of Christ. From the beginning, Christian piety, especially during the Lenten devotion of the Way of the Cross, has focused on the individual moments of the Passion, realizing that here is found the culmination of the revelation of God's love and the source of our salvation. (Prayed on Tuesdays and Fridays, and optional on Sundays during Lent.)

The Glorious Mysteries

"The contemplation of Christ's face cannot stop at the image of the Crucified One. He is the Risen One!" The Rosary has always expressed this knowledge born of faith and invited the believer to pass beyond the darkness of the Passion in order to gaze upon Christ's glory in the Resurrection and Ascension... Mary herself would be raised to that same glory in the Assumption. (Prayed on Wednesdays and Sundays.)

From the *Apostolic Letter The Rosary of the Virgin Mary*, Pope John Paul II, Oct. 16, 2002.

Prayers of the Rosary

The Sign of the Cross

In the name of the Father, and of the Son, and of the Holy Spirit. Amen.

The Apostles' Creed

I believe in God, the Father Almighty, Creator of Heaven and earth. I believe in Jesus Christ, His only Son, our Lord. He was conceived by the power of the Holy Spirit and born of the Virgin Mary. He suffered under Pontius Pilate, was crucified, died, and was buried. He descended to the dead. On the third day He rose again. He ascended into Heaven, and is seated at the right hand of the Father. He will come again to judge the living and the dead. I believe in the Holy Spirit, the holy Catholic Church, the Communion of Saints, the forgiveness of sins, the resurrection of the body, and life everlasting. Amen.

Our Father

Our Father, who art in Heaven, hallowed be Thy name. Thy Kingdom come. Thy will be done on earth as it is in Heaven. Give us this day our daily bread. And forgive us our trespasses, as we forgive those who trespass against us. And lead us not into temptation, but deliver us from evil. Amen.

Hail Mary

Hail Mary, full of grace, the Lord is with thee. Blessed art thou among women, and blessed is the fruit of thy womb, Jesus. Holy Mary, Mother of God, pray for us sinners, now and at the hour of our death. Amen.

Glory Be to the Father

Glory be to the Father, and to the Son, and to the Holy Spirit. As it was in the beginning, is now, and ever shall be, world without end. Amen.

Hail Holy Queen

Hail, Holy Queen, Mother of Mercy, our life, our sweetness and our hope. To thee do we cry, poor banished children of Eve. To thee do we send up our sighs, mourning and weeping in this valley of tears. Turn then, most gracious Advocate, thine eyes of mercy towards us. And after this, our exile, show unto us the blessed fruit of thy womb, Jesus. O clement, O loving, O sweet Virgin Mary!

Pray for us, O Holy Mother of God.
That we may be made worthy of the promises of Christ.

The Mysteries

First Joyful Mystery:
The Annunciation

And when the angel had come to her, he said, "Hail, full of grace, the Lord is with thee. Blessed art thou among women." *(Luke* 1:28)

> One *Our Father*, Ten *Hail Marys*,
> One *Glory Be*, etc.

Fruit of the Mystery: ***Humility***

Second Joyful Mystery:
The Visitation

Elizabeth was filled with the Holy Spirit and cried out in a loud voice: "Blest are you among women and blest is the fruit of your womb."*(Luke* 1:41-42)

> One *Our Father*, Ten *Hail Marys*,
> One *Glory Be*, etc.

Fruit of the Mystery: ***Love of Neighbor***

Third Joyful Mystery:
The Birth of Jesus

She gave birth to her first-born Son and wrapped Him in swaddling clothes and laid Him in a manger, because there was no room for them in the place where travelers lodged. *(Luke* 2:7)

> One *Our Father*, Ten *Hail Marys*,
> One *Glory Be*, etc.

Fruit of the Mystery: ***Poverty***

Fourth Joyful Mystery:
The Presentation

When the day came to purify them according to the law of Moses, the couple brought Him up to Jerusalem so that He could be presented to the Lord, for it is written in the law of the Lord, "Every first-born male shall be consecrated to the Lord."

(Luke 2:22-23)

One Our Father, Ten Hail Marys,
One Glory Be, etc.

Fruit of the Mystery: ***Obedience***

Fifth Joyful Mystery:
The Finding of the Child Jesus in the Temple

On the third day they came upon Him in the temple sitting in the midst of the teachers, listening to them and asking them questions.   (*Luke* 2:46)

One Our Father, Ten Hail Marys,
One Glory Be, etc.

Fruit of the Mystery: ***Joy in Finding Jesus***

First Luminous Mystery:
The Baptism of Jesus

And when Jesus was baptized... the heavens were opened and He saw the Spirit of God descending like a dove, and alighting on Him, and lo, a voice from heaven, saying "this is My beloved Son," with whom I am well pleased."   (*Matthew* 3:16-17)

One Our Father, Ten Hail Marys,
One Glory Be, etc.

Fruit of the Mystery: ***Openness to the Holy Spirit***

Second Luminous Mystery:
The Wedding at Cana

His mother said to the servants, "Do whatever He tells you."… Jesus said to them, "Fill the jars with water." And they filled them up to the brim.

(*John* 2:5-7)

One *Our Father*, Ten *Hail Marys*,
One *Glory Be*, etc.

Fruit of the Mystery: ***To Jesus through Mary***

Third Luminous Mystery:
The Proclamation of the Kingdom of God

"And preach as you go, saying, 'The kingdom of heaven is at hand.' Heal the sick, raise the dead, cleanse lepers, cast out demons. You received without pay, give without pay." (*Matthew* 10:7-8)

One *Our Father*, Ten *Hail Marys*,
One *Glory Be*, etc.

Fruit of the Mystery: ***Repentance and Trust in God***

Fourth Luminous Mystery:
The Transfiguration

And as He was praying, the appearance of His countenance was altered and His raiment become dazzling white. And a voice came out of the cloud saying, "This is My Son, My chosen; listen to Him!

(*Luke* 9:29, 35)

One *Our Father*, Ten *Hail Marys*,
One *Glory Be*, etc.

Fruit of the Mystery: ***Desire for Holiness***

Fifth Luminous Mystery:
The Institution of the Eucharist

And He took bread, and when He had given thanks He broke it and gave it to them, saying, "This is My body which is given for you."... And likewise the cup after supper, saying, "This cup which is poured out for you is the new covenant in My blood."

(Luke 22:19-20)

One *Our Father*, Ten *Hail Marys*,
One *Glory Be*, etc.

Fruit of the Mystery: ***Adoration***

First Sorrowful Mystery:
The Agony in the Garden

In His anguish He prayed with all the greater intensity, and His sweat became like drops of blood falling to the ground. Then He rose from prayer and came to His disciples, only to find them asleep, exhausted with grief.   *(Luke* 22:44-45)

One *Our Father*, Ten *Hail Marys*,
One *Glory Be*, etc.

Fruit of the Mystery: ***Sorrow for Sin***

Second Sorrowful Mystery:
The Scourging at the Pillar

Pilate's next move was to take Jesus and have Him scourged.   *(John* 19:1)

One *Our Father*, Ten *Hail Marys*,
One *Glory Be*, etc.

Fruit of the Mystery: ***Purity***

Third Sorrowful Mystery:
The Crowning with Thorns

They stripped off His clothes and wrapped Him in a scarlet military cloak. Weaving a crown out of thorns they fixed it on His head, and stuck a reed in His right hand... (*Matthew* 27:28-29)

One *Our Father*, Ten *Hail Marys*,
One *Glory Be*, etc.

Fruit of the Mystery: ***Courage***

Fourth Sorrowful Mystery:
The Carrying of the Cross

... carrying the cross by Himself, He went out to what is called the Place of the Skull (in Hebrew, Golgotha). (*John* 19:17)

One *Our Father*, Ten *Hail Marys*,
One *Glory Be*, etc.

Fruit of the Mystery: ***Patience***

Fifth Sorrowful Mystery:
The Crucifixion

Jesus uttered a loud cry and said, "Father, into Your hands I commend My spirit." After He said this, He expired. (*Luke* 23:46)

One *Our Father*, Ten *Hail Marys*,
One *Glory Be*, etc.

Fruit of the Mystery: ***Perseverance***

First Glorious Mystery:
The Resurrection

You need not be amazed! You are looking for Jesus of Nazareth, the one who was crucified. He has been raised up; He is not here. See the place where they laid Him." *(Mark* 16:6)

One *Our Father*, Ten *Hail Marys*,
One *Glory Be*, etc.

Fruit of the Mystery: ***Faith***

Second Glorious Mystery:
The Ascension

Then, after speaking to them, the Lord Jesus was taken up into Heaven and took His seat at God's right hand. *(Mark* 16:19)

One *Our Father*, Ten *Hail Marys*,
One *Glory Be*, etc.

Fruit of the Mystery: ***Hope***

Third Glorious Mystery:
The Descent of the Holy Spirit

All were filled with the Holy Spirit. They began to express themselves in foreign tongues and make bold proclamation as the Spirit prompted them.

(Acts 2:4)

One *Our Father*, Ten *Hail Marys*,
One *Glory Be*, etc.

Fruit of the Mystery: ***Love of God***

Fourth Glorious Mystery:
The Assumption

You are the glory of Jerusalem... you are the splendid boast of our people... God is pleased with what you have wrought. May you be blessed by the Lord Almighty forever and ever.

(Judith 15:9-10)

One *Our Father*, Ten *Hail Marys*,
One *Glory Be*, etc.

Fruit of the Mystery: ***Grace of a Happy Death***

Fifth Glorious Mystery:
The Coronation

A great sign appeared in the sky, a woman clothed with the sun, with the moon under her feet, and on her head a crown of twelve stars. *(Revelation* 12:1)

One *Our Father*, Ten *Hail Marys*,
One *Glory Be*, etc.

Fruit of the Mystery: ***Trust in Mary's Intercession***

This book is part of a non-profit mission.
Our Lord has requested that we
spread these words internationally.

Please help us.

If you would like to assist us financially,
please send your tax-deductible contribution
to the address below:

Direction for Our Times
9000 West 81st Street
Justice, Illinois 60458

708-496-9300
contactus@directionforourtimes.com

www.directionforourtimes.org

Direction for Our Times Ireland
Drumacarrow
Bailieborough
Co. Cavan
Republic of Ireland

+353 (0)42 969 4947 or +353 (0)42 969 4934
contactus@dfot.ie

Direction for Our Times is a 501(c)(3)
non-profit corporation. Contributions are
deductible to the extent provided by law.

The Volumes

Direction for Our Times
as given to Anne, a lay apostle

Volumes Five and Eight will be printed at a later date.

The Volumes are now available in PDF format for free download and printing from our website:
www.directionforourtimes.org.
We encourage everyone to print and distribute them.

The Volumes are also available at your local bookstore.

Appendix

The "Heaven Speaks" Booklets

*Direction for Our Times
as given to Anne, a lay apostle*

The following booklets are available individually from Direction for Our Times:

Heaven Speaks About Abortion
Heaven Speaks About Addictions
Heaven Speaks to Victims of Clerical Abuse
Heaven Speaks to Consecrated Souls
Heaven Speaks About Depression
Heaven Speaks About Divorce
Heaven Speaks to Prisoners
Heaven Speaks to Soldiers
Heaven Speaks About Stress
Heaven Speaks to Young Adults

Heaven Speaks to Those Away from the Church
Heaven Speaks to Those Considering Suicide
Heaven Speaks to Those Who Do Not Know Jesus
Heaven Speaks to Those Who Are Dying
Heaven Speaks to Those Who Experience Tragedy
Heaven Speaks to Those Who Fear Purgatory
Heaven Speaks to Those Who Have Rejected God
Heaven Speaks to Those Who Struggle to Forgive
*Heaven Speaks to Those Who Suffer from
    Financial Need*
*Heaven Speaks to Parents Who Worry About
    Their Children's Salvation*

All twenty of the "Heaven Speaks" booklets are now available in PDF format for free download and printing from our website www.directionforourtimes.org. We encourage everyone to print and distribute these booklets.

Other books by Anne, a lay apostle

Climbing the Mountain
Discovering your path to holiness
Anne's experiences of Heaven

The Mist of Mercy
Spiritual Warfare
Anne's experiences of Purgatory

Serving In Clarity
A Guide for Lay Apostles
of Jesus Christ the Returning King

In Defense of Obedience
and
Reflections on the Priesthood
Two Essays on topics close to the Heart of Jesus

Interviews with Anne, a lay apostle

VHS tapes and DVDs featuring Anne, a lay
apostle have been produced by Focus Worldwide
Network and can be purchased by visiting our
website at **www.directionforourtimes.org**

Jesus gives Anne a message for the
world on the first of each month.
To receive the Monthly Message you
may access our website at
www.directionforourtimes.org
or call us at 708-496-9300
to be placed on our mailing list.